TOY TRACTORS

Rob Wagner & Vincent Manocchi

Motorbooks International
Publishers & Wholesalers ®

First published in 1996 by Motorbooks International Publishers & Wholesalers, 729 Prospect Avenue, PO Box 1, Osceola, WI 54020-0001 USA

The information in this book is true and complete to the best of our knowledge. All recommendations are made without any guarantee on the part of the author or Publisher, who also disclaim any liability incurred in connection with the use of this data or specific details

We recognize that some words, model names and designations, for example, mentioned herein are the property of the trademark holder. We use them for identification purposes only. This is not an official publication

Motorbooks International books are also available at discounts in bulk quantity for industrial or sales-promotional use. For details write to Special Sales Manager at the Publisher's address
Library of Congress Cataloging-in-Publication Data Available

Manocchi, Vincent
    Toy tractors / Vincent Manocchi, Rob L. Wagner.
       p. cm. -- (Motorbooks International enthusiast color series)
    Includes Index.
    ISBN 0-87938-0167-0 (pbk. : alk. paper)
    1. Tractors--Models. I. Wagner, Rob L., 1954-. II. Title. III. Series: Enthusiast color series.
    TL233.8.M36   1996
    629.22' 15--dc20   95-26553

On the front cover: A child's dream—a pair of beautiful Massey-Harris toy tractors manufactured by Scale Models (top) and Ertl (bottom). The gray toy is a replica of the General Purpose (G-P) four-wheel-drive tractor built in 1932. The red model represents the large 555 that Massey-Harris offered between 1955 and 1958.

On the frontispiece: AGCO-Allis, Allis-Chalmers, Oliver, and Minneapolis-Moline are represented in a series of pewter and die-cast toys by Spec Cast.

On the title page: To get those big jobs done fast, monster equipment is required. In this case, a John Deere 8650 four-wheel-drive tractor is pulling a John Deere 550 Mulch Master. Both 1/16 scale toys were produced by Ertl.

On the back cover: The International Cub by Ertl is a 1/16 scale replica of the small tractor used for light chores on the farm. Like the real tractor, the toy features the unique "Culti-Vision" seat and International Cub graphics.

Printed in Hong Kong

CONTENTS

ACKNOWLEDGMENTS

We thank collectors Dwight Alexander of Escondido, California; and Clyde Lovitt of Romoland, California, for providing many of the toy tractors photographed in this book. Dwight and Clyde also shared their knowledge of the hobby. For their expertise and cooperation, we also thank Claire D. Scheibe, editor of *Toy Farmer* magazine; Dan Meyer of Spec Cast and Jack Potts of the Ertl Company.

The Allis-Chalmers D-21 Series II turbo-charged diesel tractor was manufactured in the late 1960s. Following a lengthy absence in marketing the Allis-Chalmers line, Ertl produced its 1/16 scale toy in 1987.

INTRODUCTION

The John Deere 140 became a very popular tool for small farms as a get-about. It also popped up around many large suburban homes as a means of quick transportation and light-duty work. This toy was made in 1966. The real McCoy was powered by a 12hp engine.

"**B**oy and Toys today! Man and Machines tomorrow!" The Minneapolis-Moline advertisement published in October 1950 remains true today. The basic foundation of marketing toy farm tractors and implements has changed little since the sales of toys mushroomed in postwar America.

But children today no longer dominate the hobby of collecting toy farm equipment. Like sports trading cards, dolls, and model cars, the art of collecting farm-related items—from the basic John Deere 620 toy tractor to belt buckles—has evolved into a multi-million-dollar industry enjoyed not only by youngsters but adults. What was once limited to toy replica farm tractors and implements has now expanded to collectible stamps, farm scenes, machinery, and finely detailed precision models.

While toy farm tractors have been on the market since the 1920s, it wasn't until the 1970s that the toys have been the object of serious collectors. The popularity of collecting anything lies in the premise that hobbyists collect what they remember as a child.

Growing up on a farm in Iowa in the mid-1950s and learning how to operate a Massey-Harris 44 tractor or visiting an uncle's farm and marveling at the workings of a wing disc or combine conjures up memories relived in toy reproductions.

Today's collectors may have no vivid recollection of the quaint Allchin 7-32 steam tractor engine or the World War I-era Waterloo Boy. As a consequence, demand for toy versions of these tractors may not be as intense as the desire to own toys of postwar models. Even youngsters today may consider a 1980s John Deere AMT 600 Transport more desirable than any toy tractor dad owned in the 1950s or 1960s.

The typical collector can't be pigeon-holed into a single category. True, the average hobbyist twenty-five years ago was the midwestern farmer or his children. And even today, most parts and

448DO
International Cub
Features unique "Culti-Vision" seat and International Cub graphics.
Size: 7.25 x 4 x 5 in.
Weight: 1lb. 3 oz.
Pack: 6

NEW FOR 1993

250DO
Farmall Super A Tractor
Size: 6 x 3.25 x 4.25 in.
Weight: 9 oz.
Pack: 6

653DO
International Cub
Size: 6 x 3.25 x 4.25 in.
Weight: 9 oz.
Pack: 6

International Cubs, for light-duty work around the farm, are featured by Ertl in a vintage tractor 1/16 scale set.

restoration shops and factory-approved dealers of toy farming equipment are based in the Midwest. But the locale of today's collector has stretched westward and eastward. There are many people lured to the hobby for a myriad of reasons.

Farming represents a romantic era to many people whether they are attracted to a less complicated lifestyle or to the intricacies of the machinery. While only a small percent of the country's population are farmers, there are perhaps thousands of people who fantasize about being in farming.

American toy tractor hobbyists typically collect 1/16 scale models—that's a miniature model that measures 1in for every 16in for a real version—while British buyers focus on the 1/32 scale. Many collectors point to the 1/16 scale as the most desirable because of the movable parts and attention to detail. Anything smaller means less detail.

While the 1/16 scale is the most popular model on the market, it doesn't preclude collectors from adding different sizes to their shelves. Most collectors focus on a single scale, but many models come in other sizes. Loads of prewar versions were scaled at 1/20. Larger scales at 1/12 still remain popular today. Most models of the Ford line were produced at 1/12 scale. Other scales include 1/25, 1/43, 1/50, and 1/87.

The manufacturing and collection of toy tractors can be broken down, and according to *Toy Farmer* magazine, toy tractors should be classified into five divisions:

• Mass-produced modern. These are toys manufactured in large numbers by hundreds of different manufacturers including the Ertl Company; Scale Models, Inc.; Spec Cast; Matchbox; and others. Even companies that produce as few as ten or more of the exact same replica for sale to the public would fit into this category.

Such toys as the International-Harvester Farmall M by Carter Tru-Scale, the Oliver 77 by Lincoln Specialties, and the Massey-Harris 44 by Reuhl are recognized as mass-produced modern toys.

• Mass-produced antique. These are toys mass-produced by such older companies as Arcade, Vindex, Hubley, Kenton, and the Kansas City Toy Company. These manufacturers constructed their toys primarily of cast-iron, diecast, or lead.

A separate category for mass-produced antique toys is critical to a collector since it would be difficult to compare the merits of any post-1950 diecast tractor to a prewar cast-iron toy.

• Customized. A customized toy is any replica that is mass-produced but altered in any way that is different from the intention of the manufacturer.

• A scratch-built modeling of a real tractor. The use of brass stock, plastic, wood, composition, and other raw materials in constructing an exact replica of a real tractor would be considered scratch-built.

Large pedal-push tractors or smaller toy tractors shaped from oak, walnut, maple, sheet metal, tubing, and/or square stock are effectively constructed from scratch.

• A scratch-built version of a uniquely designed or futuristic tractor. These types of toys are becoming increasingly popular with the growth of the toy tractor collecting industry. These toys are often modified from an existing tractor or constructed from raw materials and displaying state-of-the-art technology or projected designs of the future.

A highly popular implement offered by Spec Cast in the 1990s was the limited edition thresher with bands and chains.

Toy manufacturers in the 1920s marketed reproductions of real steam engines and tractors built during World War I. Models were constructed of cast-iron and were very crude. Detail was minimal. The Arcade Manufacturing Co. and Vindex were the most popular and consistent manufacturers of toys of that era.

Arcade was founded as the Novelty Iron Works in 1868 in Freeport, Illinois, by brothers E. H. and Charles Morgan. The company made cast-iron replicas of store fronts, pumps, and windmills before discontinuing in 1885. Arcade Manufacturing grew out of this small venture, continuing to create a variety of novelties and coffee mills until a fire destroyed the operation in 1892. Another site was purchased, and L.L. Munn joined the company as a partner the following year. Arcade flourished, producing novelties as well as coffee mills, stove pipe dampers, stove lid lifters, cork screws, and other items. It produced a line of

toys, but the toy tractor didn't make its appearance until after World War I.

The Hubley Company also was a forerunner in producing cast-iron toys. Founded in 1894 in Lancaster, Pennsylvania, the company was an early producer of highway construction equipment toys in addition to farm equipment, truck, car, and fire engine toys. By World War II, cast-iron toys were becoming obsolete given wartime restrictions and climbing transportation costs. In 1942, Hubley focused entirely on manufacturing M-74 bomb fuses.

Perhaps the most enduring toy manufacturers arrived on the scene immediately after World War II. These companies easily adapted to new materials. Ignoring the high cost of producing toys in cast-iron, aluminum, and steel, the new breed of toy companies concentrated on zinc alloy and later plastic.

The Ertl Company is perhaps the best known name in toy farming equipment. A journeyman molder in Dubuque, Iowa, Fred Ertl, Sr. lost his job in a labor dispute. It was a stinging blow to the sole breadwinner of his family of seven. Working for someone else wasn't for him.

While unemployed, Ertl noticed that John Deere was building a plant on the outskirts of town. Ertl believed that most children in the region would want a toy replica of a tractor. Drawing on his experience of making toys for his five children, Ertl and his wife, Gertrude, began manufacturing toy tractors from melted war-surplus parts, aluminum, and aircraft pistons in the basement of their home. He

RIGHT
In 1994, Spec Cast issued new 1/16 scale Ford New Holland and FiatAgri tractors with detailed engines, front weights, and moving hoods. The new items were part of a special edition.

SPEC-TACULAR News

Replica Collectables - Die Cast & Pewter

FROM SPEC CAST

Vol. 4 Number 3 - April 1994 $2.50

Two Collectable Tractors For Ford New Holland

Ford New Holland is offering it's dealers two new 1/16 scale die-cast tractors available in July. These highly detailed replicas will showcase the real model tractors which were introduced at the January, 1994, Product Show in London, England. The first is the 8970 Ford Tractor with cab which will be available with either single or dual rear wheels.

The second unit is the FiatAgri G 240 Tractor.

Both feature working super steer front axles and working flip-up hoods. Detailed cab interiors with swiveling seats and realistic consoles make these units very collectable. Also featured is a detailed engine, front weights and die-cast wheel inserts. Special paint and decals along with a die-cast collector's insert highlight these limited production run tractors. See your local Ford New Holland Dealers today and order soon as there is a limited ordering period.

1/16 Scale "SPECIAL EDITIONS"

SEE INSIDE FOR INFO ON NEW '40 FORD VEHICLE BANKS

Spec Cast's Liberty Classics ranges from a 1936 Chevrolet convertible to the company's twentieth anniversary pewter belt buckles and promotional items such as the eighteen-wheel tractor-trailer rig.

melted the metal in the house furnace and poured it into sand molds. His sons assembled the tractors while Gertrude painted them. Four years later he won a contract with John Deere to build models of their products. The Ertl Company began producing as many as 5,000 toys a day. Fred Ertl's reputation spread and he secured licensing agreements to produce toys for Case-International, Ford, Deutz-Allis, and Massey-Ferguson.

Ertl expanded his operation and moved to Dyersville, Iowa, in 1959. Production began with fifty people and 16,000sq-ft of space. By 1967, Ertl was sold to and became a subsidiary of the Victor Comptometer Corporation. Fred Ertl, Jr. became president of the Ertl Company that year as well.

Since then the plant has been expanded twice to now cover a half-million square feet which includes administrative offices and expanded production and warehouse area. Today, the Ertl Company employs 1,000 people throughout the country and has manufacturing plants in Mexico and China. It also has sales offices in Canada and the United Kingdom and a procurement office in Hong Kong. Ertl, in addition to toy tractors, also manufactures the Dukes of Hazard car, Looney Tunes mini diecast, the Batmobile, and Dick Tracy toys.

Carter Tru-Scale also began marketing its line of farm toys immediately after World War II. Founder Joseph H. Carter teamed with Fred Ertl and the Eska Company. Carter's toys, which were primarily farm implements, were marketed to complement Ertl's farm tractors. Carter produced implements for John Deere and International and truck models for International-Harvester. The company patented the free-steering type of toy tractor and sold it under the Tru-Scale logo. The company was sold to Ertl in 1970.

Arcade, Hubley, Ertl, and Carter Tru-Scale remain as the true past and present giants in toy farm tractor and implement manufacturing. Today, Ertl is joined by other companies in marketing a new line of toys. These manufacturers include Scale Models—founded by Fred Ertl Senior's son, Joe Ertl—and Spec Cast, both based in Dyersville. Other toy makers include Conrad, Revell, Monogram, NZG, Testors, Noble Toys, and C&M Farm Toys.

The art of toy tractor collecting had been limited for many years to the United States and

The Farmall 404 was an extremely popular farm tractor when it was introduced by International-Harvester in 1960. This Ertl 1/16 scale version of the tractor features plastic front wheels but diecast metal rear ones. This model has been professionally repainted

Europe. Much of the affection that hobbyists have in collecting these replicas lies in the love affair Americans and Europeans have with the automobile. Just as popular—if not more so—was the collection of toy cars, particularly Matchbox cars of the 1960s.

So it's somewhat of a surprise that Canadians have emerged in recent years as significant players in the toy tractor collecting market. While much attention has been paid to the American and European farmer, it shouldn't be forgotten that there are more than 300,000 farms in Canada and average about 525 acres apiece. In addition, nearly a half-million people are employed in agriculture.

The birth of organized Canadian toy collecting can be traced to 1970 with the founding of the Canadian Toy Collectors Society. With the moral support of several New York area collecting groups, the Canadian Toy Collectors Society flourished and soon became associated with the Motoring in Miniature Association of Buffalo, New York. By 1973, the group held its first mini-toy show in Oakville, Ontario.

Each year the toy show grew. By the 1980s it was attended by thousands of hobbyists both from Canada and the United States. It's not uncommon for top toy manufacturers, such as Scale Models, Inc.; Spec Cast; and Ertl, to appear at exhibits at the Ontario Toy Show.

Given Canada's participation and the United States' long-standing relationship with European collectors, the hobby has truly become international.

The Massey-Harris and Massey-Ferguson products are a strong line offered by Spec Cast. Note the Massey-Harris Twin-Power Challenger tractor introduced for the 1994 Louisville show.

CHAPTER ONE

1920s

Arcade made a variety of Fordsons in the 1920s. This Fordson F in original condition is not to scale, but is approximately 1/16. The red cast-iron replica of the four-cylinder tractor was purchased at a Centrailea, Kansas, dime store.

The nationwide depression of the early 1920s dampened tractor sales and forced many manufacturers to drop prices.

But novelty makers saw an opportunity to cash in on a growing phenomenon: toy replicas of automobiles, trucks, and farm tractors. While Ford, International-Harvester, and other makers scrambled to build sales, such toy manufacturers as Arcade and Vindex entered into licensing agreements to market their toy farm tractors to children of farmers.

Originally, these items were either sold or given as a promotional gimmick to children whose parents purchased the real version of the tractor. Some tractor dealers used scale models of the real tractor as a sales tool.

Nearly all of these early toy tractors were made of cast-iron. In addition to Arcade and Vindex, such companies as Hubley, Williams, Kilgore, Kenton, and Dent marketed their own versions of brand name products popular during that era.

The Ford Motor Co., which adopted and used the Fordson trademark between 1917 and 1939 (the Ford Tractor Co. of Minneapolis, Minnesota, was already founded and using the Ford name in 1916), was probably the most popular model constructed of cast-iron.

Ertl offered its version of the Fordson Model F in 1993. This Fordson, manufactured by the Ford Motor Company between 1917 and 1938, was the Model T of the field. It was a powerhouse for its day and relatively inexpensive to own. But it also was unpopular among farmers who had complained about overheating problems.

The Ertl toy version was made of diecast construction and featured the standard factory gray color of the era and bright red skeleton wheels. Fenders on the vintage Fordsons were optional so Ertl featured its version sans fenders. The '90s model of the Fordson F was only one of about a half-dozen prewar Fordsons,

This rare Arcade version of a 1920s Fordson is not to scale and was originally—and incorrectly—painted orange. This toy was made of cast-iron and typically sold in dime stores. The headless operator on these antique models are all too common.

which also included English Fordsons, marketed by Ertl.

The Fordsons also were marketed by Arcade beginning in 1928. One of its first offerings was a replica of the 1917 Fordson F. Arcade produced one F with a length of 6in and another one measuring 4in. Both sizes came in a variety of colors.

Arcade also produced a series of Allis-Chalmers tractors and a line from International-Harvester known then as McCormick-Deering. Its Allis-Chalmers models came in a variety of sizes. One cast-iron version is 3in long with the driver cast-in with the halves of the tractor. A similar model provided more

Scale Models' attention to detail has made this 1/16 scale version of the 1919 International-Harvester Titan 10-20 popular among collectors. The sand-cast toy debuted in 1993 as part of the J. I. Case Heritage Series.

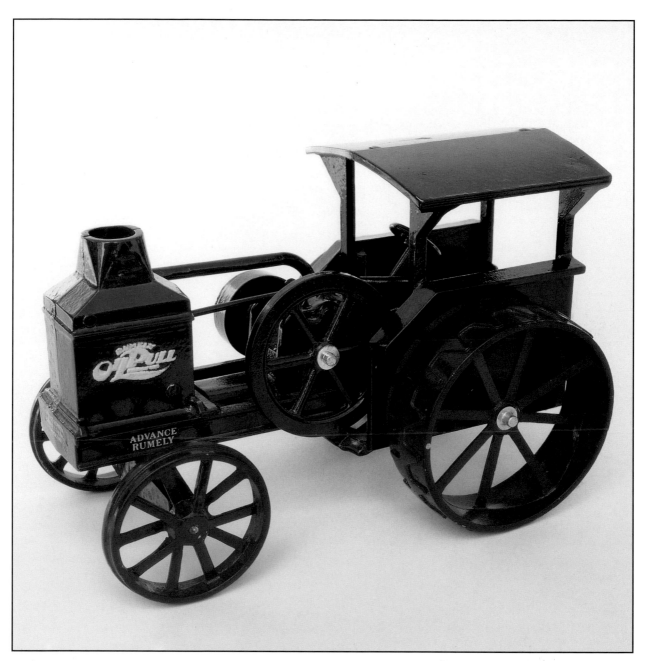

The 1919 Rumely Oil Pull, a 1/16 scale sand-cast toy, belongs to Scale Models' Thresher Series. The 1993 series also features the Case Steam Engine, Minneapolis-Moline Steam Engine, and the Hart Parr 60. This Rumely Oil Pull also comes in green.

The pre-World War I International-Harvester toy was manufactured in the 1980s by A. Ebersol of Leola, Pennsylvania, in 1/16 scale. The sand cast-aluminum toy is a limited edition.

detail and was 5in long with the company name emblazoned on the side with an accompanying bottom dump earth hauler.

An Allis-Chalmers tricycle manufactured in 1/16 scale diecast by Scale Models, Inc. also is represented.

Arcade's McCormick-Deering models featured the Farmall Original, a tractor favored by farmers looking for an easily maneuverable tractor for small row crop work. These early toys featured steel lug wheels and a non-removable driver.

In 1925 Arcade manufactured three different versions of the 10-20 model in 1/16 scale. One model featured spoked wheels while another offered cast-iron wheels with slip-on rubber tires. The third featured a red or gray tractor with white rubber wheels.

Scale Models offers 1/16 scale diecast replicas of the McCormick-Deering 15-30 and the 1923 McCormick-Deering 10-20 in a dark gray body and bright red skeleton wheels.

A desirable novelty today is the Ertl Company-produced 1915 Waterloo Boy Tractor Model R, which comes in a distinct green frame and fenders, yellow wheels, and a bright red engine. The 1/16 scale toy represents the two-cylinder, horizontal engine that sported a bore and stroke of 6x7in. The Waterloo Boy's engine was powered by kerosene fuel, and the tractor had a top speed in forward (it had a single forward speed) or reverse at 2-1/2mph. It was manufactured from 1914 to 1918 in Waterloo, Iowa, and was rated a three-plow tractor because it provided enough power to pull a plow with three 14in bottoms. The Waterloo Gasoline Engine Company, which produced this tractor, was purchased by Deere & Company in 1918.

The Model R followed several other versions. The Waterloo debuted with the TP model, then Model L and Model C, respectively. But the Model R was the only tractor reproduced as a toy.

The durable John Deere Model D, which would see service through the 1950s, was reproduced as a toy at least twice. The Vindex Company manufactured the Model D toy in the 1930s with a nickel-plated driver. Ertl came out with its version—very similar to the Vindex model—sans driver in the early 1970s. The Ertl model was painted in John Deere green and sported yellow wheels.

This tractor was John Deere's first two-cylinder vehicle to carry the John Deere name and was introduced to the American farmer in 1923. It was the most significant improvement in tractor manufacturing of the era. Deere & Company offered this tractor with about 25 percent more power than the Waterloo Boy tractor, easier maneuverability, and less weight.

A rare entry into the toy market was a limited production model issued by maker Earl Jergensen. The Jergensen 1/16 scale toy was a replica of the 1929 J. I. Case CC with a non-moving steering wheel.

The CC was Case's effort to enter into the row crop tractor business. The tractor could be converted into a cultivator by simply bolting units onto the tractor frame. The rear wheels on the real version were adjustable on the axles to accommodate various row widths.

Very few toy manufacturers of the era produced pre-1920 tractor replicas. But Scale Models, Inc. of Dyersville, Iowa, has produced an extensive line of pre-1920s tractors in recent years.

Its 1/16 scale diecast collection includes an International-Harvester line featuring the traditional green bodies and bright red spoked wheels. It highlights the 1912 IH Titan Oil Tractor, 1913 IH Moguel 12-25, 1914 IH Mogul 8-16, 1916 IH Moguel 10-20, and 1919 IH Titan 10-20.

This circa 1915 Case 10-20 manufactured by Scale Models debuted in 1993 in 1/16 scale. Scale Models is consistent in focusing many of its products on prewar farm tractors, implements, and antique engines.

CHAPTER TWO

1930s

The Fordson remained a staple of Arcade products throughout the 1930s. The unscaled four-cylinder, cast-iron replica features an operator. The Ford Motor Co. was required until 1939 to identify its tractors as Fordsons to avoid copyright infringement.

The Great Depression didn't hamper manufacturers' eagerness to build tractors with more power and less weight. As a consequence, the 1930s proved to be a decade for a lot of firsts in the industry.

In 1936, Harry Ferguson—who would merge his company with Massey-Harris in 1953 to become Massey-Ferguson—introduced his revolutionary three-point hitch system that would set the standard for years to come for hauling implements.

John Deere's styled Model A was the first tractor to be equipped with hydraulic power to raise or lower attachments. And a remodeled narrow hood on the John Deere allowed the operator excellent visibility.

Ferguson's three-point hitch wouldn't debut on toys until later in the decade. In the meantime, the toys modeled after John Deere's tractors were an immediate success on the novelty market. By the time the real styled Model A tractor was introduced in 1938, Vindex had ceased production. Arcade picked up the slack in 1940 with a 1/16 scale cast-iron version equipped with a separate plated driver, rubber wheels, and wagon option.

The styled Model A was John Deere's first concentrated effort to complement a well-engineered tractor with a touch of style. Designer Henry Dreyfuss was responsible for the new appearance which featured a new front grille and hood, enclosing the radiator and engine and giving it the "styled" designation. An unstyled tractor has the radiator exposed.

The styled Model A was a significant improvement over the so-called unstyled Model A introduced in 1934.

Ertl produced its own toy version of the styled Model A in 1946–47. It was Ertl's first toy, constructed in the basement of his home. It featured a cast-in operator, aluminum wheels, and casting webbing between the exhaust and air

Scale Models has paid close attention to prewar tractor models in recent years. This 1930s narrow row four-cylinder Fordson was built in the late 1980s in 1/16 scale and is made of sand-cast.

cleaner. When rubber became more plentiful after the war, Ertl switched to real rubber tires. The Ertl toy was again introduced in 1985 to celebrate the company's 40th anniversary. Both versions resemble the Arcade model including the hat worn by the operator.

The anniversary edition has ERTL 1945-1985 stamped on the side under the engine. Later versions came equipped with rubber tires but no driver.

Scale Models produced its version of the John Deere A in 1992. It debuted in 1/16 scale diecast with fenders.

Vindex came out with a John Deere Model D toy tractor in 1930, and it is particularly prized by collectors. Like other Vindex toys, the Model D had the operator cast separately and nickel-plated. The Vindex model was made of cast-iron in 1/16 scale and could sell today for as much as

This rare Scale Models version of the 1930s four-wheel-drive Massey-Harris was manufactured in the 1980s. At 1/16 scale, it's made of diecast metal. Massey-Harris debuted its tractors in 1917, but expanded and refined its line in the 1950s when it merged with Harry Ferguson, Inc. to become Massey-Ferguson.

$2,000. Another Model D was manufactured by Kansas Toy & Novelty in 1930 and was made of lead. It was manufactured in 1/32 scale and was of very poor quality. It's very rare, however, and still fetches a hefty price of more than $500 if in good or excellent condition. Ertl's version came in 1990 with two variations of the Model D: one with rubber tires and one with steel wheels.

Ford tractors—both the real McCoy and the toys—remained popular throughout the depression. In 1939 Ford dropped the Fordson moniker and developed the Ford 9N with a Ferguson System. Its four-cylinder 120ci L-head engine produced 28hp at 2000rpm. It was a success due to the low price and Ferguson's three-point hitch and draft control.

Arcade came out with several versions of the 9N. One of these was a 6-1/2in cast-iron model, and another was equipped with the three-point hitch. Yet another variation came with another hitch for the accompanying earth hauler. Toy maker Stanley came out with its version of the 1939 Ford 9N in 1947 and was made of sand cast-aluminum. It was virtually identical to the Arcade model.

Ford never marketed a 9N row crop model, but that didn't stop Arcade from producing a toy that was unidentified but strikingly similar to the 9N.

Scale Models produced its own version of the 1930 Fordson N model with a blue frame, raised red lettering on the radiator cover, and red skeleton wheels.

Fordson F, manufactured by the Ford Motor Co. in the 1930s, was reproduced by several toy makers, although most toy models didn't hit the market until the late 1960s.

Old Time Toys manufactured a 1/16 scale sand cast-aluminum copy of Arcade's Fordson F in 1969. Ertl came out with five versions of the model, and Scale Models offered one in 1980.

Arcade produced several different sizes of International-Harvester's Farmall M model. Some were as small as 4in long with the largest measuring 7in. Arcade's Farmall M row crop design toy came with the separate plated driver.

International-Harvester's Farmall F-20 was a durable tractor that was produced between 1932 and 1939. The F-20 at one time accounted for one-fifth of all tractors sold to American farmers. Ertl's replica enjoyed a longer run than the real tractor. It debuted in 1967 and was produced for the next twenty-four years. The 1/16 scale model featured operable steering, rubber tires, and a detailed engine. While the F-20 is given a prominent place in Ertl's history, the toy maker also produced the red Farmall F-20 in its "Precision Series" in 1993.

The Oliver Chilled Plow Company of South Bend, Indiana, had merged with the Hart-Parr Gasoline Engine Company in 1929. Hart-Parr was the first to coin the word "tractor." Tractors had previously been called gasoline traction engines.

The Hubley Company paid particularly close attention to the Oliver line. The Oliver Farm Equipment Company had been in business nearly ten years when the Hubley Company came out with its Oliver 70 series line of toy replicas.

Hubley manufactured an unusual Oliver 70 orchard tractor in 1938. This toy featured the orchard style fenders that extend over the rear wheels to protect tree branches from the wheels.

Arcade offered a replica of the Oliver 70 row crop tractor. But when Arcade ceased production, Slik Toys began manufacturing the Oliver 70 in cast-aluminum.

Arcade's Allis-Chalmers with scraper was manufactured in the 1930s and is not to scale. It's made of cast-iron. The scraper has an operating lever. Cast-iron products gave way to plastic and cast-aluminum immediately after World War II.

The orange Allis-Chalmers line was another popular group of tractors toy manufacturers tackled in the 1930s. Edward P. Allis merged with Fraser & Chalmers, Gates Iron Works (both of Chicago), and the Dickson Manufacturing Company to form Allis-Chalmers in 1901. While Allis had been involved in manufacturing steam engines since 1869, his new company began producing tractors almost immediately after the merger.

Arcade emerged with the Allis-Chalmers Model U, the tractor company's most popular and top-selling tractor. A typical Model U was powered by a four-cylinder engine with a bore and stroke of 4.375x5in and produced 33hp. Arcade's replica was only 3in long. Some versions came without the fenders and spoked-wheels found on the real models.

Allis-Chalmers introduced the Model WC in 1939 and only produced twenty-five units in its initial run. It came equipped with full two-plow power and a lighter weight to achieve greater speed. It was considered at the time the most modern tractor engineers could produce. Hubley produced a model of the Allis-Chalmers WC in the late 1930s. It was a 7in long cast-iron replica that included a driver. The Ertl Company didn't tackle the Allis-Chalmers line in earnest until the 1960s. In 1993 it offered its new Precision Series which included the Allis-Chalmers Model WC tractor. Ertl's 1/16 scale toy WC measures 8.5x4.25x4.25in

The enduring Farmall tractor was introduced by International-Harvester in 1924. It allowed farmers to use a single tractor for all purposes. This Ertl 1/16 scale replica of a Farmall F-20 features one of a long line of Farmalls offered by IH The F-12, F-14, F-20, and F-30 offered many improvements over the original Farmall. This toy measures 8x5.5x5in and weighs 1lb 15oz.

and weighs 1lb 6oz. The Scale Models version of the Allis-Chalmers WC featured steel wheels and was manufactured in 1/16 scale diecast.

One interesting toy was manufactured by Robert Gray's Pioneers of Power. This tractor represented a Allis-Chalmers Model A and was manufactured in 1971. It was made of cast-aluminum.

Spec Cast came out with the Massey-Harris Twin-Power Challenger in 1991 and 1992. The antique-style versions are gaining in popularity among many young collectors in recent years.

The 1937 John Deere G tractor was part of Ertl's fiftieth anniversary collection in 1987. It could handle three 14in plows with a drawbar horsepower of 20.70 and belt horsepower of 31.44. The G model also came with rubber tires.

RIGHT
In 1993 Ertl marketed one of its most popular and thoroughly interesting toys, the Allis-Chalmers Model WC tractor. Part of the New Precision Series for the year, the tractor measures 8.5x4.25x4.25in and featured remarkable detail in the engine area. Today, this model in pristine condition in a box can sell for more than $100.

PRECISION SERIES™

THESE CLASSIC DIE-CAST REPRODUCTIONS DEPICT TRACTORS WHICH HELPED REVOLUTIONIZE THE FARMING INDUSTRY AND REPRESENT OUR MOST HIGHLY-DETAILED PRODUCT LINE. LEVERS AND LINKAGES ACTUALLY MOVE. ALL DECAL MARKINGS REPRESENT ACTUAL TRACTOR DECORATION AND INFORMATION AREAS. EACH PRECISION INCLUDES A COIN MEDALLION AND HISTORICAL BOOKLET.

294CO
NEW 1/16 Scale Farmall F-20 (III)
Size: 8 x 5.25 x 5
Pack: 4

2245CO
NEW **Precision Series™** Allis-Chalmers Model WC Tractor
Size: 8.5 x 4.25 x 4.25
Pack: 4

Scale Models introduced this Minneapolis-Moline Comfortractor replica in 1984 much to the delight of M-M fans throughout the Midwest.

LEFT
Ertl's two toy tractors that complement each other well are the 1/16 scale Farmall F-20 and the Allis-Chalmers WC. The steering works, and the detail and decals are authentic reproductions.

CHAPTER THREE

1940s

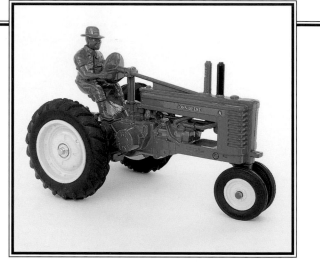

Ertl has probably popularized the collection of John Deere toy tractors with this version of the John Deere A in 1/16 scale. The toy is stamped with the notation "Ertl 1945–1985" to celebrate the company's fortieth anniversary.

The 1940s was a revolutionary decade for farm tractor manufacturers and their toy counterparts. The war years demanded more production from farmers with less manpower to feed the United States, Canada, and the war-ravaged European countries. In postwar America, tractor builders concentrated on the small farmer since about four million farmers were working less than 100 acres.

The small row crop tractor became very popular among small farmers, and the use of diesel fuel was perfected. John Deere covered both bases. It came out with the compact Model M, for small farming needs, and the Model R, which had a diesel engine. Massey-Harris introduced its smallest tractor yet—the Pony—after the war. M-H produced 27,000 units between 1947 and 1954.

On the novelty side, Fred Ertl blossomed from literally a mom-and-pop operation to the leading manufacturer of toy farm tractors. Other small concerns, such as American Precision Company and Advanced Products, came out with quality products as well.

Ertl offered a replica of the John Deere Model R in 1985. The real tractor was a bigger and more powerful tractor than the Model D

and was introduced in 1948 to meet the demands of wheat and rice growers. The introduction of the Model R featured the first successful use of diesel fuel, which had been unreliable in cold weather with difficult engine starting. John Deere manufactured a small gasoline auxiliary starting engine that helped turn over the bigger two-cylinder, 34 drawbar horsepower diesel engine.

The John Deere Model M toy was added to the Ertl line in 1989. The actual tractor was identified as a one-to-two plow tractor because it could pull a 16in bottom plow or two 12 and 14in bottoms.

These postwar rubber tractors were manufactured by Auburn and illustrate the toys' vulnerability to having the operator's head break. From left are an Oliver, a John Deere, and an International-Harvester.

One of Ertl's early products was the Farmall M, which was produced as a 1/16 scale model. The driver was cast in with the rest of the tractor. Slik Toys also produced an M model. It measured 6-1/2in long but came with no operator. Arcade, not to be left out, manufactured an M replica too. In 1940 it debuted a 1/16 scale cast-iron model with rubber wheels and a plated driver. The following year it came out with a 5-1/4in cast-iron variation. In 1942, Arcade man-

ufactured a 4-1/4in cast-iron M replica with wooden wheels due to wartime shortages.

The Allis-Chalmers WC was well represented during the 1940s. Ertl manufactured a very rare sand-cast 6-1/4in model in 1945 with either rubber or aluminum wheels and an operator. If found in excellent condition, the toy would command a top price of about $800. Arcade, however, beat Ertl to the punch with at least three separate toy versions of the same trac-

Demonstrating a brake horsepower of 58.98 and 5,674lb of maximum drawbar pull, the Massey-Harris 55 was the largest tractor of the company's line. It debuted in May 1948 but suffered from defective crankshafts. The toy is a 1/16 scale model manufactured by Ertl.

tor. In 1940, it manufactured two cast-iron toys—one at 6-1/4in with rubber wheels and the other at 7-3/8in with a nickel-plated driver. American Precision Company offered the Allis-Chalmers C in 1949. It was a 1/12 scale model that featured Goodyear tires.

Attention to Oliver tractors was divided between Arcade and Slik Toys. Arcade produced two versions of the Oliver 70 in 1940. One toy tractor measured 5-1/2in, was painted red, and featured all-rubber tires. The other version measured 7-1/2in and was painted either red or green with a plated operator. Slik manufactured replicas of the Oliver 70 and 77 in 1948. The Oliver 70 was a 1/16 scale sand cast-aluminum knock-off of the Arcade model eight years earlier while the Oliver 77 was a 1/16 scale diecast version with non-functional steering.

The International-Harvester McCormick Super M-TA featured a gasoline and diesel four-cylinder engine. The M Series was perhaps the best known tractor on American farms. Ertl's 1/16 scale replica comes in bright red, weighs 1lb 15oz, and measures 8x5.5x5in.

Advanced Products introduced a fairly well-detailed line of tractors in postwar America. Its 1/12 scale Ferguson 30, for example, featured the three-point hitch, but no implements were offered with it.

The Ford 8N was manufactured by the car maker between 1947 and 1952 and is considered one of the most stylish tractors of the era. It defined the new look that would endure for a decade. The new two-tone color scheme of cream and red for the Ford 8N was a dramatic departure from Ford's standard policy of gray-only or black-only colors. Ertl's contribution to the line came in 1987 and proved to be one of the longest running toy tractors of the Ertl stable products. It features diecast construction and authentic detailing with special attention paid to colors and graphics.

Two Oliver Super 44s were manufactured by Spec Cast in 1989 and 1990. A 1/16 scale 1989 replica was shown at the thirteenth annual Lafayette Show, and the other 1989 version was part of the Toy Tractor Times fourth in a Series edition.

Introduced in 1948, the Fleetline Series offered a powerful six-cylinder, 40hp engine. In 1949, Oliver offered Hydra-Lectric hydraulics. This toy Oliver Row Crop 77 is manufactured by Spec Cast of Dyersville, Iowa.

Massey-Harris came out with the 101 and 101 Super Row Crop models immediately before and during World War II. These tractors, popular for the completely enclosed engine compartment and streamlined bodies, are highly collectible today. This replica is manufactured by Spec Cast.

Used for small tasks, the John Deere utility tractors came in Models L and LA. Model L was introduced in 1937 and was powered by a vertical two-cylinder Hercules engine. Model LA debuted in 1941. Both models were on the market until 1946. This replica is produced by Spec Cast.

CHAPTER FOUR

1950s

The farm tractor industry had always been in a state of flux as it improved its products for the farmer each year. But the 1950s was a decade of continuing transition for the industry, moving more quickly than it ever had before. Two tractor companies, Massey-Harris and International-Harvester, emerged to grab the spotlight, and the American farmer stood up and took notice.

Harry Ferguson, Inc., finally shed the shackles of its relationship with the Ford Motor Company. Harry Ferguson had courted Henry Ford for many years to incorporate some of his inventions. It wasn't until 1936 that Ferguson perfected the revolutionary three-point hitch. A demonstration of the hitch in 1938 showed Ford that it was time to bring Ferguson into the fold. A handshake agreement between the two men resulted in a plan for Ford to manufacture the tractor while Ferguson would distribute it.

In 1946, Ford broke off with Ferguson and established a new tractor plant. Ferguson filed a lawsuit in 1948 and won a $9.25 million judgment following more than four years of litigation. Despite the judgment, Ferguson was in poor financial shape. In 1953, Ferguson merged with Massey-Harris. Briefly as Massey-Harris-Ferguson, Ltd., it quickly

The Cockshutt 40 debuted before the company's move to Canada and proved to be one of Canada's most popular farm tractors. This 1/16 scale toy is made of cast-aluminum by Scale Models.

switched to Massey-Ferguson and produced its 35 model.

In a much better financial position, Massey-Ferguson acquired F. Perkins, Ltd., of Peterborough, England, in 1958. Founder Frank Perkins had long been the leader in the industry in diesel engine design. Now Massey-Ferguson had its own engine.

Such toy makers as Advanced Products and Topping Models were devoted to the Massey-Ferguson line and put together a strong group of products for young collectors. In addition, a number of foreign toy manufacturers—including companies in South Africa and India—focused

The Massey-Harris 44 Special came with either a four- or six-cylinder engine. The four-cylinder engine was Massey's own H260 model, and the Continental F226 was used as the six-cylinder version. In all, more than 95,000 units were sold between 1947 and 1955. A four-cylinder diesel version also was offered. This 1/16 scale replica is manufactured by Ertl.

their energies on variations of the Massey-Harris, Ferguson, and Massey-Ferguson lines.

Novelty manufacturer Benbros of England, for example, produced a replica of the Ferguson 30, although the toy tractor was not clearly identified as one. Chad Valley, also of England, pro-duced the Ferguson 30 in 1955. Detail of the engine could be seen by lifting the hood, and the front wheels could be steered. Its color scheme, however, was incorrect. Chad Valley chose to paint its Fergusons green with red wheels while most of the line was painted gray by the tractor

The Ferguson 30 debuted in the early 1950s shortly before its merger with Massey-Harris. Spec Cast came out with its 1/16 scale diecast version in 1993 and was featured at the Great American Show.

company. Tekno of Denmark came out with an unusual 1/43 scale model of the "Fergie" 30 in 1954. It lacked detail like most toys of that size, but it was an interesting example nonetheless.

The Massey-Harris 33 was reproduced by Hubley as a 1/16 scale sand cast-aluminum model in 1950. It came equipped with a cast-iron operator.

Lincoln Specialties of Canada manufactured a crude 1/20 scale toy of the Massey-Harris 44 in 1950 that featured little engine detail but an unusual air cleaner and exhaust stack that could be screwed into the body. Lincoln came out with a better 1/16 scale version the same year that came with fenders, a loader, several decals, and wheel variations. The King Company, Slik Toys, Reuhl, and Dinky all offered variations of the 44 between 1948 and 1958 in diecast and sand cast-aluminum. Reuhl came up with the best replica of the 44 with a highly detailed piece.

The 1/16 scale diecast toy today sells for up to $770 in excellent condition.

PMI of South Africa manufactured a 1/38 scale model of the Massey-Harris 745D. It is highly prized by collectors today. In the United States, Scale Models, Inc. has put the Massey-Harris 333 on the market. This narrow front track version is a 1/16 scale diecast model.

The Ford Motor Co., never one to toe the line in marketing, rarely allowed a toy tractor to be made in a 1/16 scale. It declared that it didn't want its farm product to be considered the "small" tractor. The company opted to authorize production of a 1/12 scale model, although many 1/16 scale models would also be produced.

In 1953, Ford celebrated its 50th anniversary with the Jubilee model. A 1/12 scale plastic replica of the tractor with headlights was made by Product Miniature Company. The Ford 900 row crop also was replicated in plastic by Product Miniature Company in 1954. It sells today for as much as $750 in mint condition.

International-Harvester also fared well during this period developing its famous two-point fast hitch system. Toy makers embraced this new item. Manufacturers introduced replicas that featured a drawbar that could be removed and replaced with a disc or plow mounted in its place. This made the tractor and implement one integral unit.

International-Harvester also produced the Farmall Cub between 1947 and 1964. It proved to be wildly popular on truck farms and in small operations. Many of these Cubs were fitted with underslung rotary mowers for use on large lawns and in park maintenance work.

Because of its novelty, toy manufacturers seized the opportunity to ride the coattails of the

This 1/16 scale model of the Oliver Super 77 by Spec Cast typifies the late 1940s styling of this highly popular machine.

Cub's popularity. Small toy makers such as Design Fabricators, Saunders & Swader, Reuhl, and Afinson all came out with 1/16 scale plastic replicas of the Cub in 1950. Even a sand cast-aluminum model, considered very rare but manufactured by an unknown toy maker, exists.

At the other end of the spectrum, International-Harvester did not ignore the large farms. Among the larger tractors were the F-100, 200, 300, and 400 Series. International-Harvester also manufactured improved hydraulic and hitch sys-

tems. Small toy companies, like LaKone and the Marx Company, marketed versions of International-Harvester's Farmall. One example was a 1/16 scale plastic miniature of the Farmall Super C with its coiled spring seat. Today, this toy really catches the attention of collectors.

The Marx Company produced an exceptional plastic 1/12 scale model of the Farmall M diesel in the mid-1950s. The replica was accompanied by a tool box with tools and came in a wide selection of colors. The model also could

A rare McCormick Farmall 450 was manufactured in 1957 with Ertl producing its own replica the same year. It features diecast rims but a very delicate front wheel assembly. Not many of these 1/16 scale toy versions survived because they easily break. A 1957 version in the box can command up to $1,900 on the collector's market. This professional repaint version would sell for about $400 today.

be disassembled. Hubley manufactured two variations of the M in 1952. Both were made in 1/12 scale and diecast. One version had "HUBLEY" in raised letters.

Ertl came out with its International 240 in the late 1950s and featured the fast hitch and a working steering system. Other fast hitch models offered by Ertl were the Farmall 400 and 450.

Toy manufacturer LaKone focused its attention on the International-Harvester 200 and 230 models. These two replicas were 1/16 scale and made of plastic. They are considered very rare, commanding a

The son of the John Deeres A and B, the 60 model was manufactured by Ertl the same year as the real models in 1952. This 1/16 scale diecast version can fetch up to $650.

price upwards of $1,000 for an item in excellent condition.

Allis-Chalmers was well represented in toy form during the 1950s. But the replica of its HD-5 diesel crawler was manufactured only briefly in 1955 by the Product Miniature Company. It was a plastic model that featured the bright Allis-Chalmers orange color and tracks made of rubber.

The Ertl Company introduced the Allis-Chalmers WD-45 toy in 1985 for a six-year run. The WD-45 was manufactured by the tractor company between 1953 and 1957 and had an improved and advanced hydraulic lift system. Power steering was introduced in 1956. The WD-

45 was powered by a 226ci engine with a four-speed transmission. The 1/16 scale Ertl replica was part of the toy maker's "Vintage Series" and featured authentic Allis-Chalmers styling, gray air cleaner, and a narrow row crop front end.

Ertl also came out with a series of John Deere tractors with every one remaining very popular with collectors. To hail the introduction of the John Deere 60 tractor, Ertl offered its toy. Gold-plated versions were given as awards to top-selling tractor salesmen. The Model 60— introduced in 1952—was the first tractor that brought the numbered series of John Deere equipment. This model also focused on operator

LEFT
This Ertl 1/16 scale John Deere model has been professionally repainted. It features a three-point hitch with a plow. It also has steel wheels. The 620 debuted in the early 1950s and was a staple on farms for two decades. Similar to the 60 tractor, this replica is part of the 20 Series to replace the older 60 model.

convenience with an adjustable backrest, a long hand clutch, and a steering system that responded to a lighter touch. The John Deere 620 came out in 1956 and was offered by Ertl as well. It was the first toy offered with a three-point hitch. The 620 tractor accompanied the 520 and 720 models which offered different horsepower and features. A three-point hitch also was offered on the 730 John Deere toy tractor, but collectors can find a version without one as well.

The John Deere 720 high crop tractor was manufactured by Ertl in 1990 as a special edition to commemorate the Two-Cylinder Club's second antique tractor show in Waterloo, Iowa. Ertl's 430 utility tractor replica was constructed in 1958 and its 630 LP tricycle tractor was first introduced in 1988.

Ertl saluted the Ford 901 Powermaster with a limited edition 1/16 scale toy for the National Farm Toy Show in 1986. Stamped into the side of the toy is the date, "11-08-86."

CHAPTER FIVE

1960s

Pioneer Collectibles of Spring Valley, Minnesota, introduced the 1/16 scale red replica of the Canadian-built Cockshutt 770 in the late 1960s. It's made of diecast metal. The Cockshutt Co. of Belleview, Ohio, moved its headquarters to Canada just before 1960, later merging with Oliver.

It wasn't until 1960 that the Ertl Company began to pay close attention to Allis-Chalmers tractors. Ertl chose the D Series tractors to make its foray into the Allis-Chalmers line, coming out with the D Series I, II, and III. All of these miniature tractors were equipped with working steering components. As Ertl entered the second half of the decade, it released a new series of Allis-Chalmers toys, making up for all those years it ignored the tractor maker.

By 1967 Ertl released the toy B-110 and B-112 lawn and garden tractors, also with working steering systems. The B-112 version was virtually the same as the B-110 model but with a mower installed underneath the carriage and a blade attached to the front. It also provided a hitch for a trailer.

The Ertl replica of the Allis-Chalmers 190 was manufactured in 1965 and came in two nearly identical versions. The only difference between the two toys was that one model offered metal wheels while the second—released in 1966—was equipped with plastic wheels.

The toy maker produced the Allis-Chalmers 190XT and the 190XT Series III Landhandler replicas in the late 1960s. The new toys celebrated Allis-Chalmers' entry into the manufac-

turing of turbo-charged engines. XT stood for "turbocharger." The Landhandler marked Allis-Chalmers' desire for increased operator safety with a Roll Over Protection System that included an attached canopy.

Between 1987 and 1991, Ertl produced its tribute to the 1960s Allis-Chalmers D-21 Series II. The toy was a replica of the D-21 built between 1965 and 1969 and powered by a 426ci engine with a four-speed, two-range transmission that featured eight forward gears and two reverse gears. The replica is identified with a "Series II Turbocharged" decal and orange steering wheel.

Ertl announced its introduction of the 1/16 scale John Deere 3010 in 1960 when the tractor company unveiled its "New Generation of Power Tractors" line. The new series included the 1010, 2010, 3010, and the 4010. The tractors were dubbed multiple-cylinder tractors because they had four- and six-cylinder engines instead of the traditional two-cylinder engine. The line featured a streamlined hood and an emphasis on operator comfort and convenience.

The original Oliver 770 unit was built between 1963 and 1967. Spec Cast reproduced this 1/16 scale tricycle toy with rubber tires. Another version by Spec Cast is the row crop model for the "Third in a Series" category for the Oliver Collector's News.

Scale Models, Inc. produced some replicas of the 1960s Allis-Chalmers line in the early 1990s. One 1/16 scale diecast model is an excellent representation of the D17 Series I with rubber tires, chrome exhaust, and lights. Later, the 190 Bar Grill with square fenders was produced in 1/16 scale and was diecast. The real

McCoy featured a gas tank directly behind the operator's seat. Scale Models also reproduced a 1/16 scale diecast 190XT for the 1993 Farm Machinery Show.

While Ertl was seemingly occupied with producing a long line of Allis-Chalmers replicas, it didn't ignore its long-standing relationship

This 1/16 scale Ertl toy is a good example of a poor repainting job. Improper sanding and preparation leads to a very bumpy and unsightly surface. This toy was fitted with a loader. If in mint condition, this toy would sell for about $730 in a box. The International-Harvester Farmall was manufactured in 1965.

with John Deere. When the tractor manufacturer introduced the 55hp 3010 tractor in 1960, Ertl soon followed with a miniature. The 3010 had a new streamlined appearance in addition to power steering, power brakes, and a more comfortable seat for the operator.

Ertl also produced several versions of the 3020 utility tractor from 1964 to 1972. The 3020 was equipped with a 65hp engine. The row crop tractor also came with a new option: the Power Shift. The Power Shift allowed the driver to shift gears while moving under a full load. Scale Models replicated the 3020 in 1987 for the Summer Toy Festival and in 1989 for the Lancaster Show Tractor event. The 1989 model came with steel wheels.

Ertl's toy of the 2020 tractor—manufactured by John Deere in 1965—didn't make an appearance on the toy market until the early 1970s. The real tractor came with a four-cylinder, 54hp engine with three chassis, low utility, high utility, and row crop. A new slow-moving-vehicle sign was posted on the back of the operator's seat. Another replica produced by Ertl was the 5020 tractor, making its debut three years after the real model hit the market in 1966.

Ertl's John Deere standby remained the 1/64 scale 4010 row crop tractor, which was produced between 1967 and 1987. The real 4010 was manufactured from 1960 to 63 and was powered by a six-cylinder 302ci engine (the diesel version was 381ci). This miniature was among Ertl's 1/64 scale seven-piece historical set introduced in 1967. The set was available for 21 years. Spec Cast made a pewter model of the 4010 in 1/43 scale in 1990.

The Massey-Ferguson 35, left, was introduced to the American farm in 1960 and came in both the gasoline and diesel models. It was one of the first tractors to shift the load from the implement to the drawbar for added power and traction. This toy version is available at Massey-Ferguson dealers. The Allis-Chalmers 175 has a wide front end and a special display box. Both toys are diecast in 1/16 scale and are limited editions.

Ertl best represented the Ford line with the Ford 4000, which was manufactured from 1962 to 1964. Ertl replicated this model in 1/12 scale in 1965 and 1968. The 4000 was the top of the line for Ford during the early 1960s and came in either the conventional model or row crop. It had a four-speed transmission and a drawbar horsepower of 46.22. The Ertl replica featured the row crop version and came with a ribbed hood, paint, and decal scheme identical to the big version.

Hubley produced a line of Ford toy tractors during this time that rivaled the exquisite detail offered by Ertl. The 1964 Ford 6000 replica was manufactured by Hubley on four separate occasions: 1963, twice in 1964, and 1978. All were made in 1/12 scale diecast and reflected the tractor maker's new color scheme of blue and gray in

This 1963 1/16 scale Ertl model is in original condition with operable steering and diecast rims. Similar to the Case 930 Comfort King, this model features rear fenders that cover more tire area to cut down on dust.

1964. The 1964 Commander model came with an exhaust stack, but the 1978 model came without one. Hubley also offered such extras as a three-point hitch and a chrome-plated exhaust stack on its 6000 models. Hubley produced two versions of the 4000 in 1/12 scale in diecast as well.

By the mid-1960s, International-Harvester seized the opportunity to market a series of small lawn and garden tractors, which gained considerable popularity. The I-H Cub Cadets 122, produced in 1966, and the 125, manufactured two years later, greatly influenced the toy market.

This line of toys complemented Ertl's series of larger tractor replicas that would appear later in the decade. Ertl produced the Farmall 656 in two sizes. The standard 1/16

Manufactured in 1969 both by Allis-Chalmers and the Ertl Co., this 1/16 scale toy features a blade and trailer. The B-112 toy is very rare since the trailer and blades were often broken or lost over the years. To have it complete makes it a very prized possession among today's collectors.

scale offered a workable steering wheel, but the 1/32 scale miniature's steering wheel was inoperable. A toy version of the International 544 row crop tractor surfaced on the market in 1969 and offered a wide front axle with an operating steering wheel.

Ertl also started producing two more tractor lines. Following a long absence from the market, Ertl introduced the Minneapolis-Moline row crop tractor. It also began manufacturing miniature Oliver tractors in 1963, coming out with the Oliver 1800 and the Oliver 1800 four-wheel-drive units.

This 1960s toy version of the Minneapolis-Moline Liquid Propane tractor was manufactured by Hubley and is not to scale. It features all-rubber tires and operable steering.

CHAPTER SIX

1970s

White Farm Equipment and toy manufacturer Scale Models initially used silver decals on the hoods of the White 2-155 Field Boss tractor in 1979. But the logo blended in with the silver hood. So, White switched to the red decal on later models.

Anew generation of tractors emerged in the 1970s that were radically different than anything previously on the market. Operator safety and comfort became the paramount concern among manufacturers, especially when a federal law passed in 1976 required roll bars on tractors. Up until now, operators had been protected from inclement weather with canvas enclosures. These enclosures captured the heat from the engine, keeping the operator relatively warm. Umbrellas or a roll bar with a canopy became a regular feature. It was the first time in fifty years that the appearance of the standard farm tractor had changed so dramatically.

In 1979, Ford manufactured a tractor that would forever change the way tractors were designed and engineered. The TW-20 2WD was actually the forerunner to the 1980s tractor. The TW-20 had a distinctive modern look, thanks to its comfort cab. This unique tractor sported a 401ci engine and a revamped drivetrain that provided massive pulling power.

Ertl produced a toy replica of the TW-20 2WD in 1980. The 1/16 scale model remained on the market for three years and featured a molded plastic roof, diecast construction, and authentic decals and design. Like Ford, this tractor was a transitional model for Ertl with the

emphasis on fully enclosed comfort cabs offered on many of its other toy tractor offerings.

Other Ford products by Ertl included the 8600 and the 9600 models. These 1973 models were basically the same tractor, but the 9600 came equipped with a cab and dual wheels. Ertl also produced the Ford 8000 in 1970 and a 1/12 scale 4600 in 1976 that sported a flat fender design instead of the traditional rounded fenders. Another unique tractor from the Ertl line was the Ford 5550 Industrial with a loader and backhoe in a 1/12 scale.

Ertl's John Deere replicas featured the "Generation II" line in 1973. The Generation II

This 1978 model by Ertl features a black belly and operable steering and most closely resembles real the Allis-Chalmers 7045 that debuted that year. This model can sell for up to $120 in mint condition in the box.

line introduced the Sound-Gard body that adopted the design—and oftentimes the features—of the standard automobile. A John Deere Sound-Gard body provided roll-over protection for the operator with a four-post struc-ture. It had a self-contained cab with heavy insulation to keep noise and vibration inside the cab to a minimum. The operator enjoyed a posture seat, a clear view of a "control island" instrument panel, and power steering and brakes.

The Ertl John Deere 2040 was produced in 1976, the same year the real version debuted on the tractor market. Note the popular strobe decal on the side. It also features a console and operable steering.

Ertl introduced its John Deere 4430 the same time the big version hit the market in the early 1970s. The 4430 model featured a 125hp engine and complemented the other Generation II tractors, which included the 80hp 4030 and the 150hp 4630 tractor. These tractors came equipped with a full range of transmission options including a creeper transmission. While the 4430 model was popular for its "Roll-Gard" frame, nineteen toys were distributed by Ertl without the feature, making these rare versions highly prized by collectors.

The year 1976 brought a new line of utility tractors. The 2040 and 2240 utility tractors were actually manufactured in Mannheim, West Germany. The 2440 and 2640 versions were to be the last farm tractors produced at the Dubuque (Iowa) Works. While not the first tractor to roll off the German assembly line, the 2040 tractor was the first German-made John Deere product reproduced as a toy by Ertl.

Ertl also paid close attention to the Allis-Chalmers line with its introduction in 1972 of the Allis-Chalmers 200. This miniature featured front-end weights, an exhaust stack, and an air cleaner stack. Two years later, the 7040 model hit the market and featured a new design and color scheme. The Allis-Chalmers 7050 and 7069 toy

The John Deere 7520 marked the first time John Deere offered a four-wheel-drive tractor. This model was manufactured by both Ertl as a toy and John Deere as the real thing in 1972. The box on top of the cab is the air conditioning unit.

models were nearly identical with the same casting molds, but the 7050 came with a cab.

Among the International-Harvester products represented by Ertl was the rare IH 1066. It debuted in 1972 as a 1/16 scale diecast model that featured a wide front axle and roll-over protection. In 1975 Ertl came out with another version of the 1066. They both featured cabs, one in

a blue box and the other in a red box. In 1971 and 1972, the toy manufacturer came out with a very similar 966 Hydro. These toys also came in blue or red cabs. Some, but very few, were manufactured with dual wheels.

As customary with the Massey-Ferguson line, many foreign manufacturers focused their attention to the real McCoys by produc-

A rare toy version of the Case Agri King. The Spirit of '76 was manufactured by both Case and Ertl to celebration the nation's 200th birthday. Very few of these types of toys survived. And fewer real versions are seen on farms today.

ing several different toy versions. A small toy manufacturer, Minimac, came out with a Massey-Ferguson 275 that is very well detailed. Jue of South America produced a 1/43 scale Massey-Ferguson 3366 Industrial crawler in 1972. Britains, Ltd. of England pro-duced a 1/32 scale Massey-Ferguson 135 util-ity tractor in diecast metal and plastic. Scale Models marketed six different versions of the 135. One 1/16 scale diecast model in 1991 featured a horizontal stack with a collector's insert. A 1993 replica is made of brass.

Another series of tractors debuted at the dawn of the 1970s that would capture the imagination of toy manufacturers. By 1969, Minneapolis-Moline, Oliver, and Cockshutt all had merged in White Farm Equipment. A year later, several Minneapolis-Moline, White, and Oliver tractors appeared almost identical with the exception of color schemes and decals. The M-M G955, for example, was powered by a M-M engine and an Oliver drivetrain. The G955 model was first manufactured in 1973 but was marketed in Canada as a White 1870.

Between 1989 and 1992, Scale Models came out with five different versions of the Minneapolis-Moline G940 for various shows. These 1/16 diecast models, while using the basic body construction, are vastly different. One model features square fenders with a towering exhaust stack and air cleaner. Another version features narrow front wheels and no exhaust stack or air cleaner. This toy also comes with no fenders.

Scale Models celebrated America's bicentennial with the Oliver 1855 in 1976. This 1/16 scale toy with the trademark Scale Models plastic wheels is considered somewhat of an oddity by collectors. There is no specific bicentennial logo or emblem, but simply a red, white, and blue color scheme.

Ertl produced this 1/16 scale toy version of the Minneapolis-Moline G 1355 with a canopy in 1974. This toy is in original condition. Some collectors say this model is really an Oliver redecorated as a G 1355.

RIGHT
Big Bud Manufacturing of Havre, Montana, began building large tractors in the 1970s in limited numbers and costing as much as $100,000 per tractor. With a whopping 500hp, the Big Bud features dual wheels, a twelve-speed transmission, and is made to order. The toy Big Bud 500 is manufactured by Mini Big Bud of Frazer, Montana, by Martin and Karen Fast. About 300 toy units were made at about $265 apiece.

CHAPTER SEVEN

1980s TO PRESENT

Ertl manufactured its toy version of the Case International 3294 the same time the real version hit the market in 1987. This red model represents the real model that featured front wheel assist, a weighted front end, spoked wheels, console, and the orange warning sign.

As more demands were placed on the American farmer, and the need to cut costs loomed, the requirement to get the job done quicker was paramount. Farmers sought bigger machines. Comfort, safety, flexibility in the field, and durability were no longer a luxury but a requirement to stay in business.

Case International-Harvester hit the market in 1983 and 1984 with its dramatic black and white stark styling. This was set off by orange detail on the wheel rims and orange piping along the engine compartment and cab.

The 8-1/2-ton Case 3294 mechanical front-drive tractor was powered by a 504ci diesel engine and was Case's best selling tractor of the early 1980s. It featured twelve forward gears and three reverse gears. Its big brother debuted in 1984 and enjoyed a longer stint on the market. Produced from 1984 to 1989, the 4894 4WD—a member of the 94 Series—weighed 20,492lb and was powered by a 674ci engine.

Ertl honored these two behemoths with the 1/16 scale regular edition 3294 MFD that was manufactured from 1984 to 1987. The toys fea-

tured steerable wheels and the detailed black and white styling. A redesigned version was released in late 1985. The 4894 4WD was produced in 1/32 scale in 1984–1985 and featured articulated steering and rubber tires.

Case's 4994 4WD sported the standard red and black and was available to farmers in 1986. Its V-8 866ci engine had a rated gross horsepower between 213 and 400. Ertl produced a single-wheeled model of this from 1986 to 1989 in a 1/16 scale with moveable parts and plastic wheels. Toy maker Conrad reproduced a diecast version of the 4994 in 1986 in an unusual 1/35 scale.

The Ford 8970 was introduced in January 1994 and offered as a toy by Spec Cast in a 1/16 scale diecast.

Case's Magnum line was represented by Ertl with a number of toys, including the 7110, 7130, 7140, and 7150 models in either the 1/16 or 1/64 scales. The 1990–1993 Magnum MFD was first shown in Europe at the 1990 Strasbourg Trade Fair and became one of Europe's top workhorses. Ertl honored the Strasbourg Trade Fair with its copy of the 7130 for its Collector's Edition. In 1/16 scale, the toy's special features include cab windows, chrome mylar decals, the

collector's insert, and "Strasbourg" roof decal. The 7130 toy was replaced in 1993 by the 7110 1/64 scale miniature featuring solid diecast construction and new styling. It also offered an oscillating front end and moveable wheels.

Allis-Chalmers came out with its 4W-305, which proved to be one of the last tractors produced under the Allis-Chalmers name. In 1986, the company retired the name to become Deutz-Allis. The 4W-305 was built between 1982 and

producing these toys since 1985. Big Bud models 400/30, 525/50, 525/84, and 650/84 were produced by the Fasts as part of the Executive Series. Only 1,100 models are contained in each series. Top dollar on the collector market for a Big Bud in excellent condition in the box is about $400.

Ertl promoted the Deutz-Allis 6240 in 1986, which celebrated the first year Deutz purchased Allis-Chalmers. True to German technology and engineering, the real version featured an air-cooled engine.

CHAPTER EIGHT

IMPLEMENTS

John Deere's 60 tractor remained on American farms for decades and typified what the perfect tractor should be. This 1/16 scale diecast replica is featured with a loader in original condition.

Replicas of farming implements are as important to the hobbyist as the toy farm tractor itself. Most collections are not considered complete unless a combine, forage harvester, self-propelled sprayer, and similar implements are included in the set.

There is a wide range of implements represented by many manufacturers. The most common toy implements are the wagon and trailer. Two-wheeled trailers and four-wheeled wagons are perhaps the most collectible implements because of their direct use with tractors. Wagons also include flatbeds that haul packaged fertilizer, hay, rocks, and other farm products. Deep trailers usually are used to carry grain that unloads through a hopper-like chute. These wagons also are used with forage harvesters that chop corn or grass then blow it into the trailing wagon.

Farm plows also are integral to the complete collection of toy tractors and implements. Equipped with at least one but up to twelve or more bottoms, the plow kills vegetation by smothering it with dirt to hasten decomposition.

A disc, an implement consisting of several round cutting blades, helps break the soil to establish a suitable seed bed. The disc, while not as popular as the plow

or wagon, is offered by a variety of toy manufacturers.

John Deere debuted its 9600 Maximizer combine in 1989 to handle big grain, corn, and rice harvesting tasks. It produced 225hp and had a 240-bushel grain tank. Ertl introduced its replica of the 9600 Maximizer the same year in 1/64 scale and featured interchangeable corn and grain heads, movable spout, freely rotating reel, and a collector's insert to identify the toy as part of the Collector's series.

Ford New Holland came out with its 489 Haybine in 1978 and enjoyed a thirteen-year production run. It featured spiraling chevron rolls that cracked the crop stem lengthwise then crimped it every three to six inches for uniform drying. Ertl's 1/64 toy version didn't hit the

Arcade was one of the first toy manufacturers to produce replicas of farm implements. This unidentified 1920s cast-iron 1/16 scale thresher is in original condition.

market until 1988. It featured a hitch, freely rotating reels, tires, and rollers.

Ertl's version of the Deutz-Allis R50 gleaner combine was produced in 1/64 scale and was marketed from 1987 through 1992. The R50 Gleaner combine was one of several self-propelled gleaners that was manufactured from 1987 to 1991. It featured a 200-bushel grain bin and a 190hp engine. The Ertl toy offered many moving parts, interchangeable grain/corn heads, and a moveable spout. It's authentic styling and graphics makes it extremely popular among collectors.

Ertl's collection of John Deere implements is extensive. John Deere debuted the 9000 Series combine in 1989 and Ertl came out with its replica a year later. The self-propelled six-cylinder, turbocharged diesel sports up to 260hp. The 9000 Series came in three models, the 9400, 9500, and 9600. The 1/64 scale model offered interchangeable corn and grain heads, moveable spout, and a freely rotating reel.

Older toy John Deere combines include the New Generation Combines of the early 1970s: the 300, 400, 6600, and the 7700. The 6600

Arcade came out in the 1950s with a 1/32 scale postwar version of the Minneapolis-Moline Model U with combine, disc, plow, planter, and manure spreader. These versions are made of cast-aluminum.

combine debuted in 1970 and featured a fully exposed reel and auger chaindrive. Ertl came out later with the gear drive shielded.

The Titan line was introduced in 1979 and featured combines with a higher threshing capacity, wide headers, and more powerful engines. The first Titan toy combine to hit the market was not equipped with a stop on the header. When the toy was lifted off the ground, the header dropped down. Subsequent versions of the Titan corrected this flaw, making the original replica highly prized. The Titan II toy came out in 1985 with a green cab top that replaced the standard yellow top on previous models. The decals also were changed.

Spec Cast produced several different versions of implements over the years that have attracted new attention from hobbyists. Spec Cast's high quality replica of the unique John Deere 6500 self-propelled sprayer with a narrow front end is a 1/16 scale diecast model. The real version was manufactured at John Deere's plant in Ankeny, Iowa. The toy is part of Spec Cast's Limited Collector's Edition and is packaged in a collector box. It measures 46in wide with the booms open, 8-3/4in tall, and 13in long.

Another Limited Special Edition by Spec Cast is the 1/28 scale diecast McCormick-Deering thresher from J. I. Case. It is patterned after the 28x46in separating bed size of the real version.

Stephen Mfg. of Beloit, Wisconsin, came out with its intricate John Deere 77H five-bottom moldboard plow in a 1/16 scale. It is made of cast metal with rubber tires and breakaway couple and hitchpin.

Slik Toys debuted its Oliver 70 and combine in 1946 in 1/16 scale. This cast-aluminum replica was a dealer promotion item. The tractor, missing the operator, has been repainted. The combine is in original condition.

Scale Models, Inc. has always been a leader in manufacturing a wide range of toy implements. Popular among collectors are the Deutz-Allis orange three-piece implements. This set featured a utility wagon, disc, and a five-bottom plow individually packaged in a display box. All are constructed with diecast metal frames.

In 1/64 scale, Scale Models, Inc. featured its steam engine and separator set. The steam engine came in a green, black, and red color scheme while the separator was painted in silver with red wheels and trim.

Part of the J. I. Case Heritage Series are the 1/24 scale International-Harvester buckboard wagon in a white and red color scheme and the

1/24 scale Case buckboard wagon with a green and red combination.

Scale Models, Inc. also produced a diecast 1/16 scale N-6 combine, which is considered rare by collectors and is valued up to $235 if in mint condition and in a box.

During the first half of the 1950s, Massey-Harris enjoyed unprecedented attention by several small toy manufacturers. Such toy makers as Reuhl, Lincoln, King, and Eisele produced several 1/16 scale implements in cast-aluminum, plastic, and diecast. In 1950, for example, Lincoln manufactured a Massey-Harris flare box wagon, a mower, and a disc. All met with varying degrees of success on the toy market.

Gone are the plastic farm scenes of yesterday with little detail. Ertl has developed a series of sets that include everything from electronic sounds to a whole barnyard full of animals.

Pewter belt buckles allow the collector to wear his hobby. The collector can also place the buckle on a shelf or in a display case with his most prized toy tractors. Spec Cast of Dyersville, Iowa, has long been a powerhouse in farm- and transportation-related novelties before manufacturing toy tractors. The toy manufacturer has produced a long series of belt buckles featuring anything from the standard farm tractor to limited editions commemorating specific events and anniversaries. The company introduced its

Spec Cast offered its Heartland Toys featuring the 1993 Farm Show Edition of the Oliver 77 in 1/64 scale.

"Pewter Collectible Series" in 1988 that featured replica 1/43 tractors. A year later it debuted the Liberty Classics diecast replica vehicle banks.

Pedal tractors made a tremendous comeback in the late 1970s as a collectible. State and national tractor pulling races were formed in 1982 and come close to rivaling toy tractor shows as one of the most popular aspects of the hobby. Hundreds of children from as many as twenty-seven states and provinces in Canada participate in annual pedal tractor pulling contests.

Collecting pedal tractors and competing in organized races introduces children into the hobby. Most competitions are divided into age groups ranging from four- to twelve-year-olds. Pedal tractor pulls are very similar to the real tractor pulls, but pedal-power by children is the only way to cross the finish line.

Pedal tractor manufacturers were primarily limited to Eska and Ertl. Eska manufactured a number of Allis-Chalmers pedal tractors in the 1940s and 1950s. Its 34in 1949 Allis-Chalmers C can fetch up to $750 in excellent condition. Eska also produced several Case pedal tractors through 1958. The company even made two-wheeled trailers to complement the tractors. One version features flare-sided fenders and another was built with straight-sided fenders.

Highly prized by collectors are Eska's Oliver 88 pedal models. Manufactured in 1947 and measuring 33in long, Eska offered two separate 88s—one with an open grille, the other with a closed one. The open grille model commands a top price of about $1,300 while the

SpecCast ™

Heartland

FARM MACHINERY

DIE·CAST METAL

Oliver 77
Narrow Front

'93 Farm Show Edition

Stock #95002

85

A wide range of toys by Spec Cast features an unusual Terra-Gator 1603, rotary mower, and an antique gasoline engine along with the more common eighteen-wheeler and 1/64 scale tractors.

closed grille version can sell for about $1,100 in excellent condition. Two-wheeled trailers also came with these models.

Ertl offered 39in pedal Olivers in such models as the 1800, 1850, and 1855 between 1962 and 1972. Ertl's Massey-Ferguson line of pedal tractors debuted in the 1970s with a variety of 37in models.

Perhaps the most reproduced tractor moniker is the International-Harvester with dozens of versions manufactured between 1949 and the late 1980s. Jumping into the IH pedal tractor fray were Eska, Inland, Ertl, and Scale Models.

Between 1953 and 1958, Eska came out with several pedal versions of the Case tractor. Ertl also produced pedal Case tractors including an attractive 1982 36in model with a unique strobe decal. Trailers by both Eska and Ertl complement the pedal versions.

John Deere pedal tractors have been on the market since 1949 when Eska introduced its first 34in Model A in sand cast-aluminum. It featured an open grille and came only in red. It can command a top dollar of more than $3,000 in excellent condition. Eska went on to produce pedal tractors for John Deere models 60, 620, and 730 in sand cast-aluminum. They were mostly 38in in length. It also produced trailers for the John Deere and even an umbrella to shade the youthful operator. Ertl produced pedal replicas for a wide variety of John Deeres, including the 3650 and 4020.

SPEC-TACULAR News
Replica Collectables - Die Cast & Pewter
FROM SPEC CAST
Vol. 3 Number 3 - APRIL 1993 $2.50

AGCO Adds Collectables To Line!

AGCO is introducing some very collectable units to it's line of collector products. The first is a 1/16 scale die-cast Minneapolis Moline "U" Collectors Edition Tractor, **AGCO 003.** This limited edition unit features the famous M-M orange color with red rims and rubber tires. The front headlights and steering wheel are black. It also has a chrome muffler and a painted air cleaner.

The second unit is an Allis Chalmers black and orange Vega Airplane Bank, **SC35023.** This is the first airplane bank in their series. This plane features the original Allis logo on the fuselage. The third unit is a yellow and green Oliver Travel Air Airplane Bank, **SC40008.** The Oliver logo is on the wing and "Oliver Farm Equipment Co." is on the fuselage. The two planes have twist-off cowls to remove your coins and the cockpit cover lifts off to reveal the coin slot. See more AGCO items in this issue.

SEE PAGE SIX FOR "COLLECTING" FEATURE ARTICLE

Clockwise from lower left, the John Deere B was ideal for small farmers. Built from 1935 to 1952, it was rated at 9.28 drawbar and 14.25 belt horsepower. The John Deere 55 Series model was introduced to the American farmer in 1989. New models replaced the 50 Series. The John Deere 630 LP tractor was popular among farmers who lived near oil refineries where liquid petroleum was cheaper than gasoline or diesel. The four-wheel-drive 8020 diesel was equipped with an eight-speed transmission and built between 1960 and 1964. These replicas are manufactured by Spec Cast of Dyersville, Iowa.

LEFT
Spec Cast in recent years has emerged as stiff competition to Ertl in the toy tractor market. Spec Cast not only specializes in toy tractors but a line of other toys that go hand in hand with the tractor. Airplane banks, for example, feature authentic Allis-Chalmers and Oliver logos.

CHAPTER TEN

RESTORATION

Since the early 1980s, the number of original mint condition toy tractors has diminished greatly as more and more collectors scour the flea markets and toy shows for the perfect replica.

There is something to be said for keeping a piece in original condition, even if it has peeling or chipped paint, broken or missing parts, or scratched decals. But more collectors today are restoring their toys to mint condition for many reasons. The foremost concern of a hobbyist is whether a certain toy is available in the condition desired. A miniature may be so rare that the only way a collector can add one to the display case is to refurbish it. Restoration techniques also have improved greatly over the years. Replacement parts are better, painting techniques have improved, and skilled toy restorers are more easily accessible.

Having a toy tractor or implement professionally restored is becoming more popular. Farmers in particular perform this type of work during the winter as a way to earn some extra money. A typical job can cost about $20 for labor and the price of parts. Total cost for an average job ranges from $50 to $60. The toy will be undercoated, painted, and have new rivets and tires installed.

Yet, professional restorations can devalue a toy considerably. Many manufacturers paint their toys on an assembly line. The same spots on every toy are missed by the spray painter or receive only a light coat. A professional restoration is much more thorough but also easily recognizable as a restored item and not original.

Restorers should examine the decals of the toy to determine whether they should remain or be replaced. If the old paint shows through the decal, it may be best to apply new ones after a paint job. But if the decal is in good shape, it can be masked off when the toy is repainted.

So when does the condition of a toy tractor reach a point that it would be better to refurbish it? Beauty is in the eye of a beholder. It depends on the tastes of the collector. To consider a collectible toy tractor in good or even excellent condition, no more than 20 percent of its paint should be scratched or chipped. Some toys in well-used condition are attractive simply because they are "well used." But if that chipped or scratched paint detracts from the overall appearance of the toy, it probably should be repainted.

It also should be noted that in many instances repainting a cast-iron toy may be the best way to preserve its value. Unrestored cast-iron toys in excellent condition are extremely rare. These types of toys are generally in poor to only fair condition so refurbishing would be the best option.

The following steps should be taken for proper home restoration of a toy tractor:

1. Preparation and stripping. If a total paint job and decal replacement is desired, the old paint and decals should be stripped to the bare metal. Improper stripping or sanding of old paint gives the new finish a blotchy or uneven look.

Rubber tires should be removed by submerging the wheels in warm water. Paint can be removed by carefully sanding with fine-grained sandpaper, although it's difficult to get into the engine compartment or other small crevices. The use of a chemical paint remover is more thorough and oftentimes easier to use. Sandblasting is another option to remove paint and decals but is expensive.

2. Masking. Standard masking tape from a hardware store is the best tool to mask portions of a toy not to be painted or to prepare for a two-tone job. The edge of the tape should be firmly attached to the surface to prevent paint from bleeding onto another area. A razor blade or hobby knife can trim along fine edges.

Templates made from paper or cardboard is perfect for shielding some paint, but the user should be careful of overspray.

3. Painting. For the best results, painting with a hobby air brush or small compressor is suggested. However, pressurized spray cans also give a professional look. Directions from the can should be followed explicitly. Spray painting the toy should be done in even strokes.

It's imperative that the proper colors be applied to tractors. Painting a John Deere tractor a bright red instead of the traditional trademark green would make the toy worth less.

And any green won't do, just like any orange paint won't fit an Allis-Chalmers. The wrong shade of paint on a toy standing in a long line of correctly painted items stands out like a sore thumb. The proper shade of paint should be pur-

chased from toy tractor distributors or even from dealers of the real McCoy.

4. Applying decals. Replacement decals have become more available to toy restorers in recent years. Flea markets, toy shows, and dealers usually have a wide assortment of decals for the most popular tractors.

Older versions may be more difficult to track down although many collectors painstakingly repaint logos, trademark labels, and marquees.

For those collectors not so artistically inclined, professional silk screeners can do the job but at a significant cost.

Applying a decal is a simple task if patience is exercised. Simply submerge the decal in room temperature water for less than one minute then apply it to the area desired. Smooth over the decal with a damp sponge to eliminate water bubbles. A light touch is necessary to avoid tearing or creasing the decal once it's on the surface of the toy.

Many older toys made of cast-aluminum or cast-iron have raised letters and numbers of the manufacturer and model number. A detail brush, rubber roller, or rubber blotter should be used to apply the paint.

Indented letters or numbers on such toys can be applied by putting paint on the tip of a finger then forcing the paint into the depressions. Excess paint on the edges can be wiped away before drying.

CHAPTER ELEVEN

PRICES

The value of a toy tractor is dependent upon the price agreed between the buyer and seller. While price guides are available for the serious collector, determining the value of toys is an individual matter. What's worth hundreds of dollars to one collector may be of minimal value to another. It's all a matter of taste.

But to help the hobbyist become competitive in the art of buying and selling toy tractors, basic guidelines must be followed to determine the proper price for an item. Value is generally broken down into three categories: good, excellent, and in the box.

When determining the value of a toy tractor, the following should be considered:

• Condition. A dented or scratched toy will diminish the value of a tractor considerably, but it still may command a high price depending on the item. A well-used 1/16 scale Allis-Chalmers D-21 will not command much money. But a damaged early Arcade version of a Fordson or McCormick-Deering might if it's a rare item and difficult to obtain.

Many postwar models have easily accessible replacement parts. Damaged or cracked rubber tires can be replaced. Logo or icon decals also are available for replacements. Yet, if a tractor is in need of repair and no replacement parts are available, value drops. If a toy has as much as 20 percent of its paint missing, it still may be considered an object in good condition. A toy in excellent shape must have no chips or scratches on the paint and looks as though it had just been removed from the box it was shipped in.

Cast-iron toys are rarely found in good or excellent condition. The criteria for judging such a replica in good or excellent condition is more strict. To have a cast-iron item rated in excellent condition, less than 5 percent of its paint can be missing.

• Professional repaints. A good professional repaint job on a toy will allow the owner to sell it at a competitive price. Owners should be warned, however, that a poor or even a good paint job will devalue the toy. An excellent paint job will probably ensure a good price for the toy, but it will rarely—if ever—increase its value.

A professional repaint job can never make a toy climb in value, simply because the repainting will probably be a better job than the factory work. At a factory, each toy receives the exact same paint job, because they are painted on an assembly line. A repaint job is easily spotted because the quality is usually better, and the

John Deere 60 with combine.

individual attention to painting nooks and crannies are not apparent on an assembly line model. It's the imperfect factory paint job that makes the toy attractive.

Repainting cast-iron toys adds little or no value since these replicas are generally worth less than diecast or cast-aluminum toys.

• Quantity. Toy tractors manufactured over a period of several years are not as valuable as a limited edition model. An Oliver bicentennial model manufactured on a one-time basis in 1976 is far more marketable than a John Deere tractor that enjoyed a six-year run by the Ertl Co. Thousands of John Deeres may be on the market while that limited edition Oliver, being much more rare, commands a higher price.

Ertl often produces limited edition models to commemorate specific farm and toy shows. These special edition toys are often stamped with the name of the show and date, enhancing its value.

• Boxed toys. These toys are perhaps the most valuable and sought-after items at toy tractor shows. Untouched and unwrapped toy tractors in a box command huge prices. A 1940 Allis-Chalmers WC with a nickel-plated operator that was manufactured by Arcade can sell for nearly $2,000 if in mint condition and contained in the original box. A 1982 Ford 7710 in a box may sell for only $20.

The toy tractors listed below represent a cross section of the hobby. It is not a complete list. Prices listed are for toys in excellent condition unless otherwise noted.

Allis-Chalmers WC by Arcade
1940 6-1/4in cast-iron with rubber wheels—$211
1942 6-1/2in cast-iron with wooden wheels and two-piece driver—$206

Allis-Chalmers D-21 by Ertl
1987 1/16 scale diecast collector series—$51
1988 1/16 scale diecast Minnesota State Fair special edition—$80

Allis-Chalmers Model U by Scale Models, Inc.
1992 1/16 Louisville Show tractor series—$51

Ferguson Model 30 by Spec Cast
1993 1/16 scale diecast The Great American Show Series—$42

Ford 9-N by Arcade
1941 6-1/2in cast-iron—$431

Ford 9-N by Ertl
1989 1/16 diecast with plow and insert 50th Anniversary Ford 9-N 1939–1989—$46
1993 1/64 scale, No. 8 in Toy Tractor Times Series with silver hood—$48

International-Harvester 10-20 by Arcade
1925 1/16 scale cast-iron with spoke wheels—$1,438 in box
1925 1/16 scale cast-iron with cast-iron wheels and slip-on tires—$1,493 in box

International-Harvester 10-20 by Kilgore
1925 1/20 scale cast-iron—$1,200

International-Harvester 240 by Ertl
1959 1/16 scale diecast fast hitch utility—$1,413

International-Harvester 886 by Ertl
1976 1/16 scale diecast with roll-over protection shell—$118 in box

International-Harvester 966 by Ertl
1971 1/16 scale diecast with white front wheels—$168
1972 1/16 scale diecast with red box—$144
1972 1/16 scale diecast with blue box—$206

John Deere A by Ertl
1946 1/16 scale sand cast-aluminum with open flywheel lights—$299
1947 1/16 scale sand cast-aluminum with closed flywheel—$163

John Deere 60 by Ertl
1953 1/16 scale diecast with taillight on seat—$276

John Deere 630 by Ertl
1958 1/16 scale diecast—$475
1959 1/16 scale diecast, gold-plated (rare)—$833

John Deere 2040 by Ertl
1976 1/16 scale diecast utility—$75
1980 1/16 scale diecast with loader—$14

John Deere 4430 by Ertl
1972 1/32 scale diecast—$12
1973 1/25 plastic—$31

Massey-Ferguson 175 by Reindeer
1978 1/16 scale diecast with Goodyear on tires—$354

Massey-Ferguson 670 by Ertl
1983 1/20 scale diecast with front weights—$18

Massey-Harris 33 by Hubley
1950 1/16 scale sand cast-aluminum with cast-iron driver—$453

Oliver 77 by Slik
1948 1/16 scale diecast—$269
1952 1/16 scale diecast—$426
1954 1/16 scale diecast with open engine and green wheels $521

INDEX